How to CARE for Works of ART on PAPER

By FRANCIS W. DOLLOFF, Chief Conservator

and ROY L. PERKINSON, Assistant Conservator

Department of Prints and Drawings

Museum of Fine Arts

Boston

ISBN 0-87846-055-1
Library of Congress Catalogue
Card No. 77-157703
Reprinted March 1972
Typeset in *Trump Medieval* and printed
by Thomas Todd Co., Boston
on Mohawk Superfine Softwhite, 80 lb.
Designed by Carl F. Zahn

Contents

Preface 5

1 The History of Papermaking 7

2 The Enemies of Paper 13

3 Matting and Framing 25

4 A Note on Restoration 35

Materials and Services 41

Bibliography 45

Preface

Paper is taken for granted. Why not? It is cheap, available, and expendable. At the same time it is indispensable and yet poorly understood, and it is the need for understanding, with particular reference to works of art on paper, that is the subject of this booklet.

The publication of this guide was prompted by two exhibitions held at the Museum of Fine Arts, Boston, in the spring of 1971: "The Art and Craft of Papermaking," organized by the Library of Congress, and "Conservation of Works of Art on Paper," organized by the Museum's Conservation Laboratory of the Department of Prints and Drawings. The material is based on our experience in dealing with the countless queries that have come into the Conservation Laboratory from private collectors, galleries, museums, libraries, historical societies, and even artists and framers concerning prints, drawings, watercolors, pastels, books, manuscripts, and documents. A basic explanation of the nature of paper and an enumeration of the fundamentals of preservation, including framing and matting, are brought together in a single convenient source of practical information. Perhaps a few readers will be encouraged to delve still further into the subject by consulting the works listed in the selected bibliography that follows the text.

It is no secret that the problems of displaying, framing, storing, transporting, and preserving works of art on paper are legion. Unless solutions are readily accessible, there is a danger that these graphic records of our historic and artistic heritage will not survive far into the future. It is important that the characteristics of such important records be understood.

Everyone of us, inside or outside museums, and whether or not we are directly concerned with conservation, has a personal interest at stake in the little-understood subject of paper. For example, think for a moment of the pictures on your wall or of those stored, unframed, in your attic with its intense summer heat, or, worse still, in your cellar with its warm-season dampness and its cold-season dryness. Think of the books on your shelves in full sunlight or over a heat register, their leather bindings suffering from dryness and lack of nourishment. Finally, look at irreplaceable letters, or other valuable manuscripts, the writing bleached into illegibility by strong light and the paper fragile from much folding and unfolding. Most people will recognize one or more of these conditions in their own home.

This guide will have served its purpose if it enables a wider audience to recognize the make-up and characteristics of paper and to understand the qualities that ensure permanence and the care that is necessary for the longevity of even the best and most durable papers.

We wish to express our gratitude to Mohawk Paper Mills, of Cohoes and Waterford, New York, for their technical advice on modern printing papers and for their financial assistance in the preparation of this booklet and installation of the Conservation Laboratory's exhibition "Conservation of Works of Art on Paper."

For their encouragement, advice, and assistance in the preparation of this booklet we also thank Eleanor Sayre, Curator of the Department of Prints and Drawings, Diggory Venn, Special Assistant to the Director, Margaret Jupe, Assistant Editor, and the staff of the Department of Prints and Drawings.

F.W.D.

R.L.P.

1 · The History of Papermaking

Paper is such a commonplace of twentieth-century life that one rarely pauses to reflect that the material that makes up today's newspapers, books, prints, certificates, cups, plates, napkins, and countless other objects for dignified or humble use had its origins nearly two thousand years ago. According to tradition, this amazingly versatile material, whose importance for civilization is scarcely less than that of the wheel, was discovered in 105 A.D. by an ingenious Chinese eunuch named Ts'ai Lun. Like so many great inventors, Ts'ai Lun seized on an idea that was simplicity itself. He sought a use for the scrap cuttings of the expensive woven cloth then used for writing. He beat the scraps until they were reduced to a mass of individual fibers, mixed the mass with water, and poured it onto a cloth or bamboo screen. The water drained away leaving behind a matted sheet of fibers – paper! The basic process of making paper by spreading a slurry of fibers onto a porous screen has remained unchanged in principle down to the present, in spite of the enormous changes in the mechanics of accomplishing this act.

Ts'ai Lun's followers found that paper could also be made from bamboo, hemp, and mulberry bark. The Japanese, for example, who began making paper in the seventh century, relied primarily on mulberry bark. Even today, the Japanese "rice paper" sold in art supplies stores is made not of rice but of mulberry bark.

Conquest and caravans brought paper and the secret of its manufacture to the West via Samarkand, Baghdad, Egypt, and Morocco, and by the twelfth or thirteenth century Spain and Italy had begun making paper. The process underwent a few minor changes during this long journey, since the Chinese materials were not available, and paper was in competition with parchment as a writing material. The early European papermakers macerated cotton and linen rags for fibers, and to keep the ink of the quill pen from feathering or bleeding out into the sheet they dipped the paper into a tub of warm gelatin (an extract from the hoofs, hides, and horns of animals), which gave the paper a harder surface. This process is known as sizing. The amount of sizing in paper depends upon its eventual use. Writing paper requires a hard surface and therefore a large amount of size. Printing paper requires less, and blotting paper almost none.

Instead of using a bamboo screen, the Europeans fashioned their paper molds from metal wires stretched across a wooden frame, a simple device on which paper was made for all the books, drawings, and prints produced in Europe for many centuries. The skilled craftsman dipped his mold into a vat of fibers floating in water, lifted it, and by just the right series of to-and-fro motions gently formed the sheet of paper. The "vatman" was the key individual in the papermaking business: the ability to make a uniform sheet not only once but time after time required long years of apprenticeship as well as physical endurance. After the vatman had formed each sheet, an assistant transferred it to a heavy felt, gradually building a pile of felts and paper sheets in alternation. This pile was then placed in a large press, which forced out excess water and consolidated the sheets of paper. After sizing, the paper was sent to the drying loft and draped over long ropes to dry.

Since so much skilled labor was involved in papermaking, it is not surprising that the manufacturer soon began to take special pride in "branding" his paper with his own watermark in the form of his name, insignia, or a special design. The watermark is produced by a thin wire pattern attached to the screen of the paper mold. Since this design projects above the surface of the mold, the paper is thinner wherever it has touched the wire. The translucent mark is visible when the paper is held up to the light.

Gutenberg's invention of movable type in the fifteenth century firmly established the usefulness and necessity of paper. From then on the papermaker struggled to keep pace with demand and faced two ever present difficulties: the cost of labor and the scarcity of raw materials. Mechanical and chemical innovations helped to solve these difficulties but also posed new ones. Technology improved quantity at the expense of quality.

The Hollander machine, named for the country in which it was invented, was one of the most important of these innovations – a seventeenth-century version, one might say, of the modern food blender. Metal blades cutting and churning at high speed in a large tub of rag cuttings mixed with water quickly reduced even the toughest of rags to a smooth, even pulp. The Hollander soon replaced the enormous stamping machines whose heavy, pounding hammers had previously been used for pulping the rags. The shorter fibers produced by the Hollander resulted in a weaker sheet of paper but produced fifty to a hundred times more pulp than the stampers.

Another seventeenth-century innovation was the introduction of alum (potassium aluminum sulphate), a chemical used to harden the gelatin size and to keep it from putrefying while in the tub. Alum soon became one of the standard papermaking materials, with unfortunate results for the strength and longevity of paper. It has been found that alum radically increases the acidity of paper.[1] From the second half of the seventeenth century onward, use of this chemical severely diminished the strength and permanence of writing papers, and only in recent times has its destructiveness been fully recognized and corrected.

The disastrous effects of chlorine, use of which began in 1774, were realized more immediately. It was employed as a bleach for stained or colored cloth, previously deemed unusable for book and writing paper, and it caused entire stacks of paper to crumble into dust before they could even be used.

The supply of rags never seemed to catch up with the demand for paper, which by the nineteenth century had become enormous. In the latter part of that century, an ingenious papermaker in Maine, I. Augustus Stanwood, conceived the idea of "importing mummies from Egypt for the sole purpose of stripping the dried bodies of their cloth wrappings and using the material for making paper."[2] The woven wrappings and papyrus filling were transformed into a coarse brown wrapping paper which was eventually used by grocers for wrapping vegetables, meats, and other foodstuffs! An outbreak of cholera among the ragpickers and cutters in the mill, probably from contact with these disinterred Egyptians, seems to have put a stop to this enterprising plan.

The search for an economical substitute for rags long occupied papermakers. By 1800 as many as 135 substitutes had been suggested, including asbestos, thistles, potatoes, linden leaves, St. John's-wort, corn husks, cabbage stalks, and cattails. Eventually wood showed the greatest promise. Its potential as a papermaking substance had first been suggested in 1719 by the French scientist René Antoine Réaumur, who had been impressed with the ability of wasps to make paper nests from wood. In 1800 Matthias Koops published in London a book of which a part was "printed on paper made from wood alone . . . without any intermixture of rags. . . ."[3] Koops was ahead of his time and was unable to capitalize on his invention, but within a few decades practical methods were devised for grinding and pulping wood.

The first groundwood pulp mill in the United States was founded near Stockbridge, Massachusetts, in 1867, and the very next year the first New York newspaper to use groundwood pulp was printed. Today newsprint and groundwood pulp are virtually synonymous. Anyone who has seen his old newspaper clippings disintegrate within a few years will not need to be convinced that groundwood pulp paper can be of poor quality. It is weak largely

1. See William J. Barrow, *Permanence/Durability of the Book,* Richmond, Va., 1963–1969.
2. Dard Hunter, *Papermaking,* 2nd ed., New York, 1967, p. 382.
3. Hunter, *Papermaking,* p. 332.

because its preparation produces extremely short fibers in clumps and retains a large amount of the binding material (lignin) that held the fibers together within the tree. This binding material breaks down easily into acidic components, which attack paper and cause it to deteriorate.

The wonder is that, despite the use of all these destructive agents by the papermakers, any books or works of art on paper should have survived at all. Fortunately, these materials and methods were not used uniformly by all papermakers. While some mills turned to assembly production of magazines, newspapers, and inexpensive books, other mills were less "progressive" and stayed with traditional methods, continuing to produce high-quality papers for the artist and fine printer. It thus came about that there became available a great variety of papers with widely different qualities of permanence. Today it is possible for a contemporary artist like Robert Rauschenberg to obtain paper just as fine as that used by Audubon for his *Birds of America* (1827–1838). At the same time, it is equally possible for the unwary artist to use paper that will scarcely outlast an ordinary newspaper. Similarly, the art collector may find that the mat he so admired has seriously stained the picture it was supposed to protect; or the librarian may find that many recently purchased books have become unusable.

What is the lesson to be learned from these facts about paper? First, we must learn to be discriminating in our use of paper. The paper must be suited to its purpose: if permanence is required, then the quality must be chosen accordingly. The traditional handmade papers of Europe and the Orient will answer the needs of special users, such as artists. For those who run today's high-speed printing presses, however, the critical technical requirements for uniform thickness and weight, special sizing, and large quantity rule out these traditional types of paper. But the papermaking industry has learned a great deal from the mistakes of the past and can now write a prescription for longevity that modern technology can administer.

The ideal combination for permanence seems to be an acid-free and alum-free pulp made of the purest possible fibers – a condition that, ironically, was essentially fulfilled by the ancient papermaking methods, although by circircumstance rather than design. The purest papermaking fibers available in quantity to the modern papermaker are pure, new cotton and pure high-alpha cellulose. A paper made with these fibers and without acidic ingredients may be said to be highly permanent and durable, free from the causes of internal deterioration.

To help to control the external factors that affect permanence, some fine, acid-free text papers have been made with available alkali present, which acts as a buffer to neutralize any possible acid contamination from handling by the user or reader or from the atmosphere in which the paper is kept. Artificial aging tests carried out on paper made with pure high-alpha cellulose and alkaline additives have indicated an expected permanence in excess of three hundred years. Anyone concerned about the future of paper can now take heart, whether it is a matter of reading a favorite novel again in a few years time or of preserving a valuable picture for the next century.

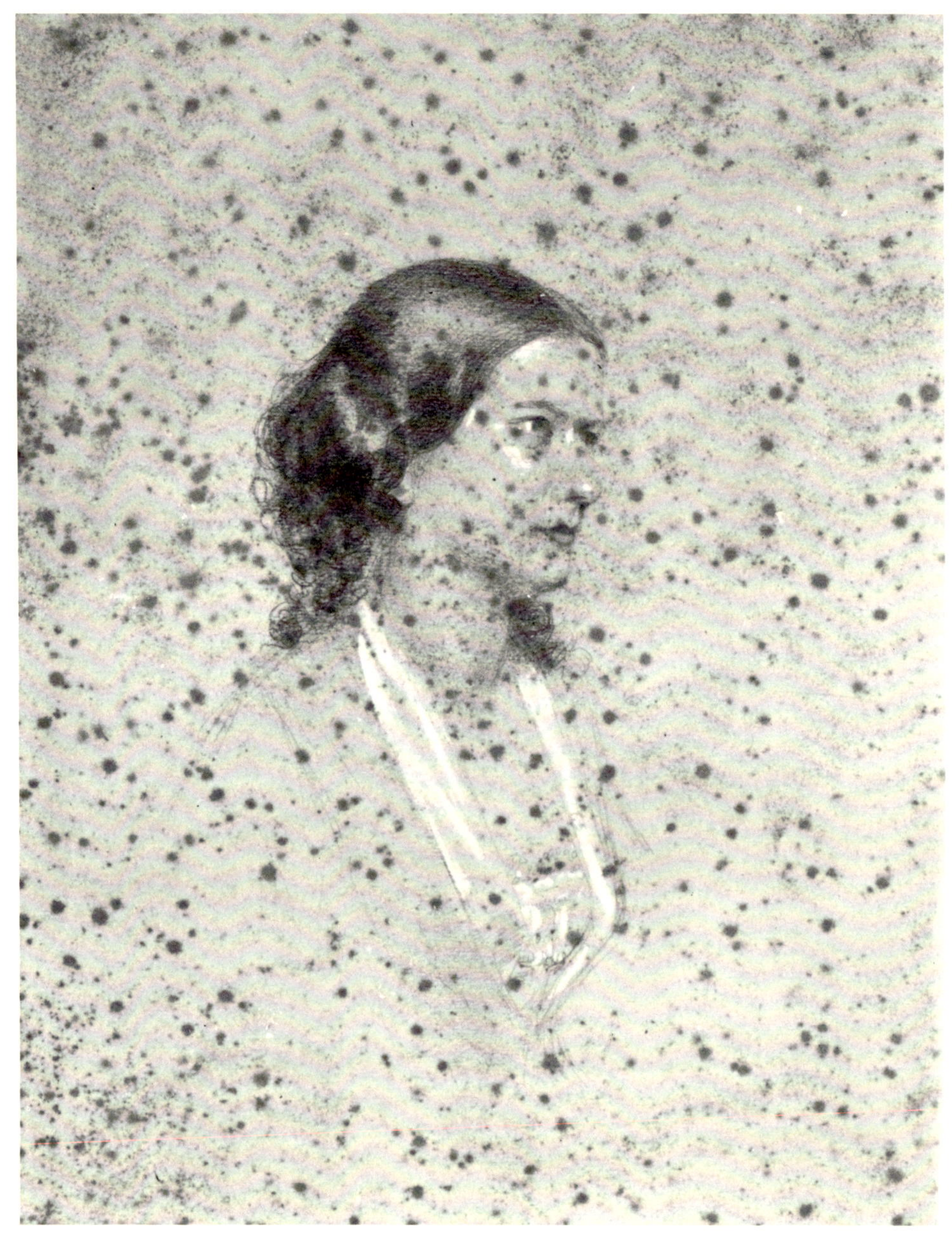

1 *Mold growth caused by excessive humidity resulted in the foxing on this pencil drawing.* GEORGE FULLER (1882–1884), *Portrait of a Lady.* M. AND M. KAROLIK COLLECTION.

2 · The Enemies of Paper

Paper is fragile. Although it can last for centuries if properly made and cared for, it is highly susceptible to damage by environmental conditions, by insect pests, and by man. But dangers may also come from within, for paper may begin with flaws.

INHERENT FAULTS

Even the finest handmade papers are sometimes disfigured by stray pieces of wood or rusty metal, marks from the ropes in the drying loft, or buckling caused by hasty drying and curing. Much more serious defects can result from the various technical "improvements" mentioned earlier. Machines were devised for preparing pulp composed of shorter and shorter fibers, which made a weaker sheet of paper. Chemicals used to make a whiter sheet from a larger range of raw materials were so harsh that strength was further reduced. Incomplete washing and the addition of still other chemicals, particularly alum, left dangerous residues that, like an invisible time bomb, ensured eventual destruction.

Of course, there are now many types of paper that are by nature short-lived, that are born to die. The newspaper or paperback book, for example, will not be in readable condition for more than a couple of decades, perhaps less. But then, should they be? On the other hand, many book publishers and libraries have awakened to the fact that, because so little attention has been paid to the built-in dangers to paper, the majority of books printed in the first half of this century – books that *should* last – will probably be unusable by the year 2000. This alarming situation has impelled modern technology to answer the question of what constitutes paper permanence, so that one can at least choose whether the paper to be used will last long enough to suit the purpose. Thus, the present situation differs from that in the fifteenth century in that permanence in paper is now a matter of choice rather than of circumstance.

Use of a permanent paper is half the battle of preservation. If publishers want their product to last, they should select paper with the appropriate specifications. Artists should seek out the many fine all-rag papers available if they want their work to outlive them. Art collectors should take care to see that only all-rag mats and acid-free papers are used in framing their pictures (see "Matting and Framing"). Archivists, librarians, and curators should familiarize themselves with the acid-free papers and storage materials existing today.*

HANDLING

Most damage to paper caused by man could be avoided with just a little extra care and common sense. The standard rules of handling are as follows:

1. Use clean hands to handle books and pictures.
2. When lifting matted or unmatted pictures, use *two* hands to keep from bending, creasing, or tearing them.
3. Unmatted pictures should never be stacked directly on top of each other but should be separated by a smooth, nonacid cover tissue.*
4. For optimum protection valuable pictures should be matted rather than left loose. Less valuable pictures or documents can be kept in acid-free folders or envelopes.*
5. Be careful not to touch or drag anything (the corner of another mat, for example) across the surface of a picture. Mezzotints, pastel drawings, and silkscreen prints are particularly vulnerable to surface damage.
6. Never use pressure-sensitive tapes (Scotch tape, masking tape, etc.), gummed brown wrapping tape, rubber cement, synthetic glues, or heat-sealing mounting tissue on any picture that is to be preserved.
7. Pictures glued down on old boards should be handled with as much care as any unmounted, brittle picture. The backing gives a false sense of strength, which may put one off guard.
8. Matted pictures should be protected with cover tissue* when not in use. For temporary display or protection, the entire mat can be wrapped in a cellulose acetate* sheet and secured with tape on the back, but this material should not be used for permanent storage because of its dust-attracting static electricity.
9. Open a mat by the outer edge, not by inserting a finger through the window and lifting the inner edge.
10. Pictures in mats or folders can be stored in drawers or solander boxes.* Wooden drawers and cabinets are preferable to metal ones, since the latter can condense moisture inside and will quickly transmit heat in the event of fire.

*Materials marked with an asterisk are listed in the section "Materials and Services."

11. To carry, mail, or ship loose pictures, pack them flat between stout boards, not in a roll.

ENVIRONMENT

Humidity

The chief danger of excessive humidity is the growth of mold. Since mold cannot grow unless the humidity exceeds seventy percent, preventive measures must include keeping the humidity below that amount. Air conditioning or dehumidifying machines are the answer in moist climates and damp buildings. For airtight containers and exhibition cases silica gel,* a dehumidifying agent, may be helpful (see Nathan Stolow, *Controlled Environment for Works of Art in Transit,* London, 1966). When hanging or storing pictures beware of dampness on outside walls in stone houses and in basements and cellars. Houses closed up for an extended length of time may become excessively humid and should be aired periodically and checked for signs of dampness or musty odors.

To illustrate the damaging effects of poor ventilation we mention a colored woodcut recently brought into the Conservation Laboratory that had mold growing not only inside its frame but also all over the outside. It had hung in a summer home that had been closed during the winter. And as a further example, two fine eighteenth-century engravings were treated for mold growth that had resulted from five years' storage in a warehouse without adequate circulation of air.

Mold growth in paper often shows up as dull rusty patches that discolor the sheet. This is called "foxing" and is caused by the chemical action of mold on the colorless iron salts present in most paper (Figure 1). Mold feeds on sizing and paper fibers and thereby weakens the sheet. It also grows easily on pastels, which contain good nutrients for mold in their binding media. Foxing is the usual result of prolonged, high atmospheric humidity, but if water itself seeps into the picture or book, rampant proliferation of mold may completely envelop the object. First-aid treatment is to remove the object to a dry environment. Open the frame or spread out the pages so that air can circulate freely to the infested areas. Expose to direct sunlight for about one hour to kill the mold or, preferably, place in a closed container with some crystals of thymol,* a fungicide, for two or three days.

Small sachets or dishes of thymol crystals placed in bookcases or storage containers can help to prevent mold. Librarians and art collectors may also want to construct a thymol cabinet designed specifically for treating mold. It should have a metal floor on which the thymol crystals are placed and several racks or shelves on which pictures and books can be spread out to allow the thymol fumes to permeate the paper. The metal floor is gently warmed from below by low-wattage bulbs (forty-watt), which are turned on every day or two for about an hour to make the thymol crystals volatilize more effectively. The placement and power of the bulbs should be adjusted so that the metal floor *never* feels hot. If evaporation occurs too quickly, the thymol vapors may saturate the air in the cabinet, recondense as small oily droplets, and form spots on the pictures. Since thymol softens oil paint, the inside of the cabinet should be left unpainted. For the same reason pictures painted in oils should never be treated with thymol.

Since thymol is volatile, it offers no permanent protection against recurrence of mold if an object is returned to a humid environment. For example, the surface of a pastel painting recently brought into the Conservation Laboratory was covered with mold. A note on the back of the frame indicated that the pastel had been treated for mold fifteen years earlier, and the owner revealed that after treatment it had been put back in the very same place as before, on the damp outer wall in an old stone house; thus it had contracted another bad case of mold.

In summary, the rules for guarding against mold are as follows:

1. Keep the humidity below seventy percent; about fifty percent is ideal.
2. Do not store pictures or books in damp cellars or basements.
3. Avoid hanging pictures on the outside walls of a house, especially if they feel cold or damp.
4. Never frame pictures directly against the glass (see "Matting and Framing"). To do so invites damage by mold growth or condensation of moisture.
5. Clean bookshelves, frames, and storage areas regularly, as dust contains a large amount of air-borne mold spores.
6. Good circulation of air reduces chances of mold growth.Circulation of air behind a frame is improved by attaching small pieces of cork or wood to the lower two corners to keep the frame away from the wall.
7. Never store pictures or books directly on the floor. Raise them on supports to allow circulation of air.
8. Avoid leaving books and pictures in a closed room or house for extended periods of time without providing some means of circulation or dehumidification.

9. Fumigate infested books, pictures (except oil paintings), storage containers, and bookcases with thymol fumes to kill mold, and be sure to correct the conditions that originally caused the mold growth.

Light

Of all the external factors that can affect paper, light – perhaps because it is so much a part of our everyday experience – is often the most ignored and misunderstood.

In times past, prints and drawings were traditionally kept in books or albums as illustrations to texts and shown now and again in the parlor to gatherings of family or friends on Sundays or special occasions, much in the way albums of snapshots are shared today. Life styles have changed, and today the print or drawing is made to serve as a decoration on the walls of a house, office, or gallery, a function that often exceeds its original purpose. Furthermore, the growing interest in art has not only spread ownership of prints and drawings but has also augmented the number of exhibitions and hence the accessibility of these works of art. The net result is a drastic increase during the last several decades in the danger of damage resulting from overexposure to light.

Collectors, rightly concerned with this hazard, often ask conservators whether fading can be stopped by keeping watercolors, drawings, or colored book bindings in subdued light. Unfortunately, and to their surprise, the answer is "no." It must be remembered that *all* light fades works of art on paper; less light means only less fading. Pigments used by the papermaker to tint his product or by the artist to create his image do not automatically stop fading when the light drops below a certain level (see Figure 2). And fading is not reversible. Placing a work of art on paper in darkness merely halts the process and does nothing to promote recovery or rejuvenation.

How much light should be used for viewing works of art on paper? What minimum amount of light does the human eye need to perceive all colors in their proper relationships? The answer is one of degree. Anyone who takes a walk by moonlight can verify that when light is at an extremely low level the eye loses all ability to perceive colors and can only distinguish tonal, or black and white, values. Therefore, one can only conclude that there must be sufficient light for good viewing, but any excess, which will hasten fading, must be avoided at all costs. An optimum amount of light is five foot-candles, which corresponds roughly to the output of one 150-watt reading lamp at a distance of three or four feet. In other words, use the same amount of light for viewing works of art on paper as is required for casual reading.

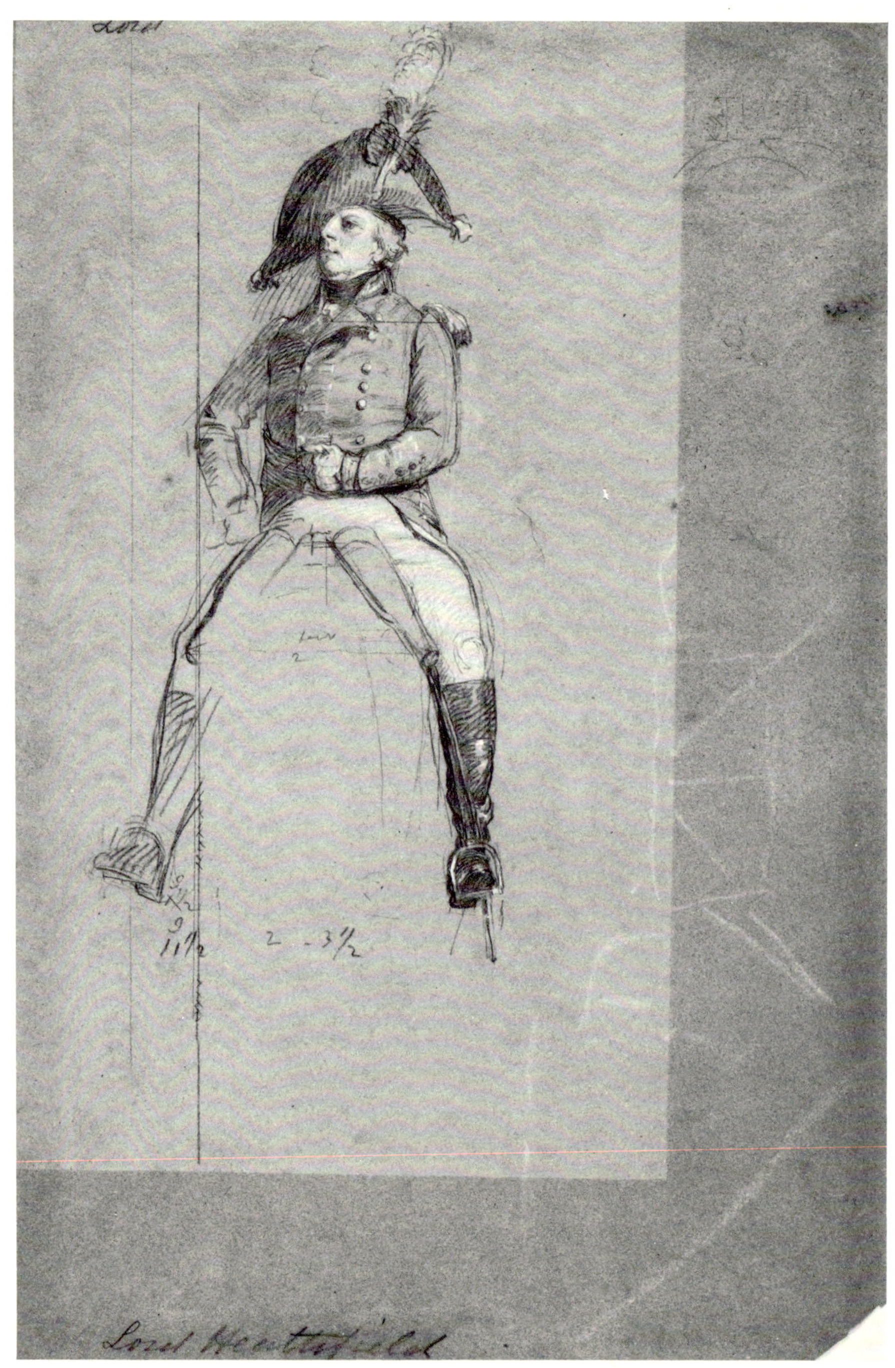

Bear in mind that the human eye is a poor judge of light quantity because it adapts so easily to major changes in intensity. The eye needs mechanical assistance to make an objective determination of light quantity. This can be accomplished quite simply with an ordinary photographic light meter, like the Weston, which is callibrated in foot-candles. Follow this procedure. Take a sheet of white blotting paper or other similar unglazed white paper, at least one square foot in size. Put the paper in the position that the picture is to occupy and, following the manufacturer's directions for using the meter, make a reading of the light reflected from the sheet of paper. The proper amount of light is now determined.

The next step is to guard against unnecessary exposure. Museums and historical societies control exposure by various means. It is their practice, for example, to keep delicate watercolors and documents with fading ink in storage for viewing only by appointment. They display them in rooms lit artificially only during well-defined hours. They install them in cases protected with fabric coverings, which the visitor himself can remove and replace. In the nineteenth century, some Victorian frames for watercolors were equipped with a small curtain, resembling a window shade, that would roll up inside the molding when raised to view the picture.

Most large museums rotate selections from their holdings so that an object is never left on view for more than a few months at a time, a practice which even the modest collector might well emulate. Simply changing the position of the pictures in your house once every year or so will not only diminish the possibility of their fading but will place them in a new perspective that will enhance enjoyment of them. The established collector might even consider the possibility of storing a certain percentage of his collection on a rotating basis.

Avoid hanging pictures or placing bookshelves or glass-fronted bookcases on a wall directly opposite windows, since the light is likely to be greater there than anywhere else in the room. Translucent curtains or louvered blinds can be used to moderate or redirect the bright light of day.

Pictures should, of course, never be hung in direct sunlight. Even reflected or indirect daylight, however, carries a danger in addition to intensity, for it is

Facing page:

2 *The fine blue paper used for this chalk drawing was badly and irreversibly faded not by direct sunlight but merely by exposure for ten years to indirect morning light reflected from within a room. The original mat covered a large area on the right and bottom of the sheet and protected this from fading.*

J. S. Copley (1738–1815), Study for *George IV, when Prince of Wales.* M. and M. Karolik Collection.

a source of ultraviolet light, which, though invisible, is even more destructive than visible light. Ultraviolet rays accelerate fading and even cause deterioration of the paper itself. Watercolors, prints, drawings, and books should therefore never be exposed directly to these damaging rays. Fluorescent lights are a potent source of ultraviolet light and should always be covered with cylindrical plastic sleeves* that filter out the dangerous radiation. Alternatively, Plexiglas sheets,* which effectively filter out ultraviolet light, may be substituted for glass in a picture frame (see "Matting and Framing").

Heat

Do not expose pictures and books to heat, since high temperatures accelerate the deterioration of paper. Do not hang pictures over a radiator, heating register or air duct. That enticing spot above the fireplace is doubly bad as a place to hang pictures, first, because of heat, and, second, because soot and gummy residues produced by the fire adhere to the glass and obscure the picture.

Air Pollution

Urban areas are antipaper. The city dweller should realize that a polluted atmosphere is one of the dangers that threaten the longevity of paper and the permanence of works of art on paper. The most harmful contaminant in the atmosphere is sulphur dioxide, a gas produced by combustion of fossil fuels like coal and oil; it is a major constituent of smog. Sulphur dioxide attacks paper and causes discoloration, embrittlement, and eventual disintegration of the paper fibers. It is absorbed by the paper and converted into sulphuric acid, a particularly strong acid that does not evaporate and leave the paper even after it has been removed from contact with the gas. Severe brown stains caused by this destructive pollutant are often seen on framed pictures that have been partly or entirely exposed to the air by lack of adequate backing (see Figure 3). Sulphur dioxide also robs leather bookbindings of their strength and pliability and can eventually reduce them to mere powder. At the turn of the last century library holdings were severely damaged by the high concentration of sulphur dioxide produced by the use of illuminating gas.

Certain artist's pigments can also be affected adversely. Ultramarine blue, for example, which is often used in watercolor painting, can be completely destroyed long before the paper itself has been even moderately discolored. White lead, encountered more often in oil paintings but sometimes used as a

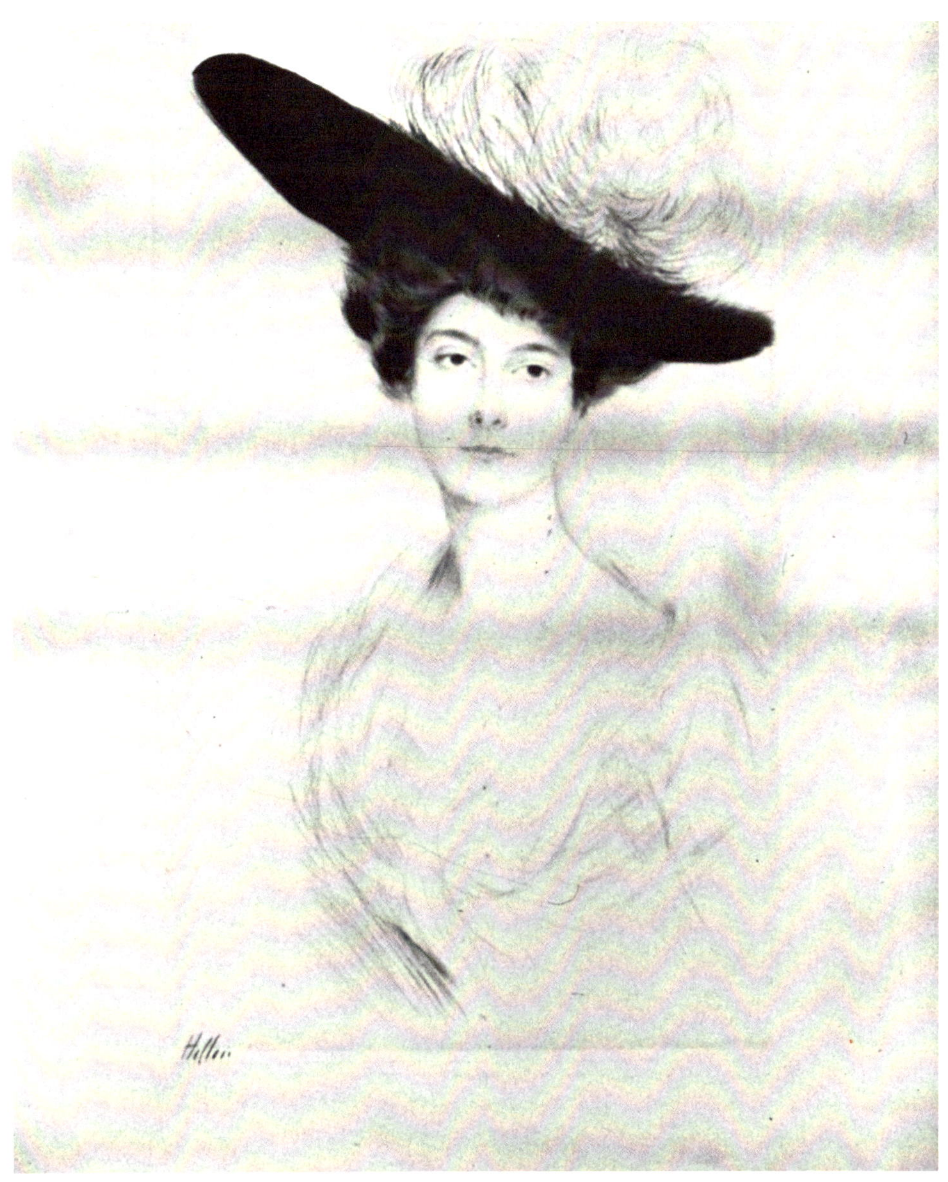

3 *The framing of this engraving in direct contact with a four-piece wooden back resulted in staining from wood resins and from sulphur dioxide, which seeped through the openings in the back.*
PAUL HELLEU (1859–1927), *Woman with a Hat.*

highlight or as body color in wash drawings or watercolors, reacts with sulphur dioxide to form lead sulphide and darkens to a dirty gray or sooty black, thereby destroying the tonal range of the picture.

Air pollution seems to be an inescapable hazard of urban life. The only sure defense, short of removing the paper to the relatively uncontaminated air of the suburbs or the country, is to install air conditioning. The restorer can help to minimize the effects of pollution by washing or deacidifying paper that has been exposed too long to city pollutants. Protection of framed pictures with all-rag board, front *and* back, plus a backing large enough to cover the entire mat will help to minimize danger from a polluted atmosphere. The new technology is also introducing into paper manufacture alkaline chemicals which aid in neutralizing the damaging effects of pollutants. Acidic substances which attack and destroy leather bookbindings can be neutralized by applying a solution of potassium lactate.* (For directions on applying this solution see Carolyn Horton, *Cleaning and Preserving Bindings and Related Materials,* 2nd ed. rev., Chicago, 1969.)

Insects

The most common insects that threaten paper are silverfish, termites, cockroaches, and woodworms. Silverfish are silvery, or pearl grey, insects with three tail-like appendages; they are often discovered when books, papers, or frames on the floor are picked up or suddenly moved. They prefer warm, damp places, shun the light, and move so quickly that detection is difficult, so that they may cause considerable damage before they are noticed. A serious threat to books, they are equally damaging to works of art on paper. They will eat their way through pictures to get at flour paste and glue sizing but also enjoy bleached wood-pulp paper (see Figure 4). A picture about 16 by 20 inches in size was brought into this laboratory for treatment; its surface had been almost entirely devoured by silverfish, so that scarcely a trace remained of the original image.

Although termites and woodworms are commonly thought of as enemies of wood alone, they will devour virtually anything made of cellulose, including paper. Their winding, branching tunnels can cause considerable structural damage to book covers, frames, and pictures that have been mounted on wooden panels (see "A Note on Restoration").

Cockroaches inhabit dark, warm, damp places, and usually come out during the night. They cause surface damage to parchment, leather, paper, fabrics, and any glues or painting media containing sugar. Infestation by these insects is best prevented by regular cleaning and by inspection of the dark spaces

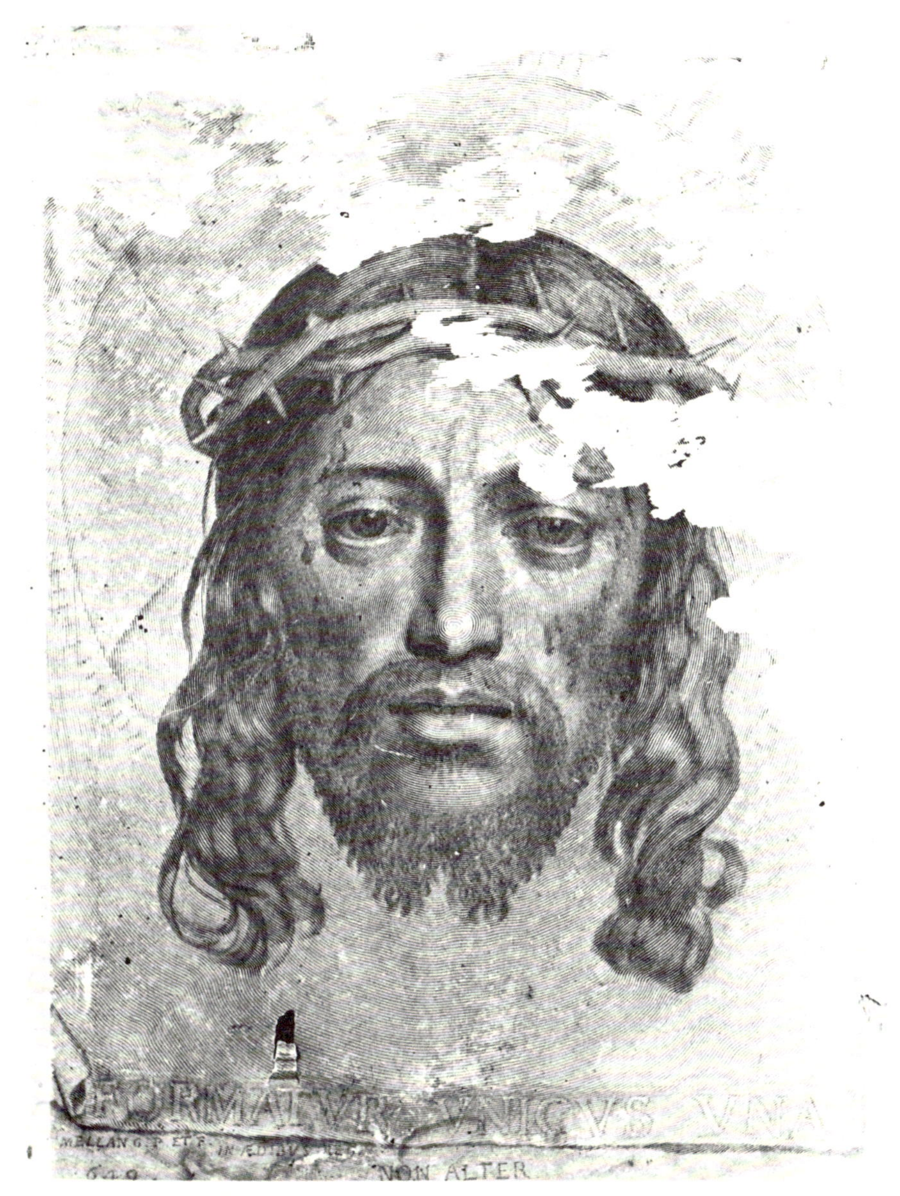

4 *Silverfish virtually destroyed this engraving while eating the gelatin sizing in the paper and the glue used for mounting.*
CLAUDE MELLAN (1598–1668), *The Sudarium.*

behind and beneath books, cases, boxes, and picture frames. Particular attention should be paid to areas such as basements and attics, where traffic is minimal, and which tend to be damp or dark. Use of aerosol or powdered insecticides is necessary if signs of these insects are present. (For further information see Cunha, *Conservation of Library Materials*, Metuchen, N. J., 1967.)

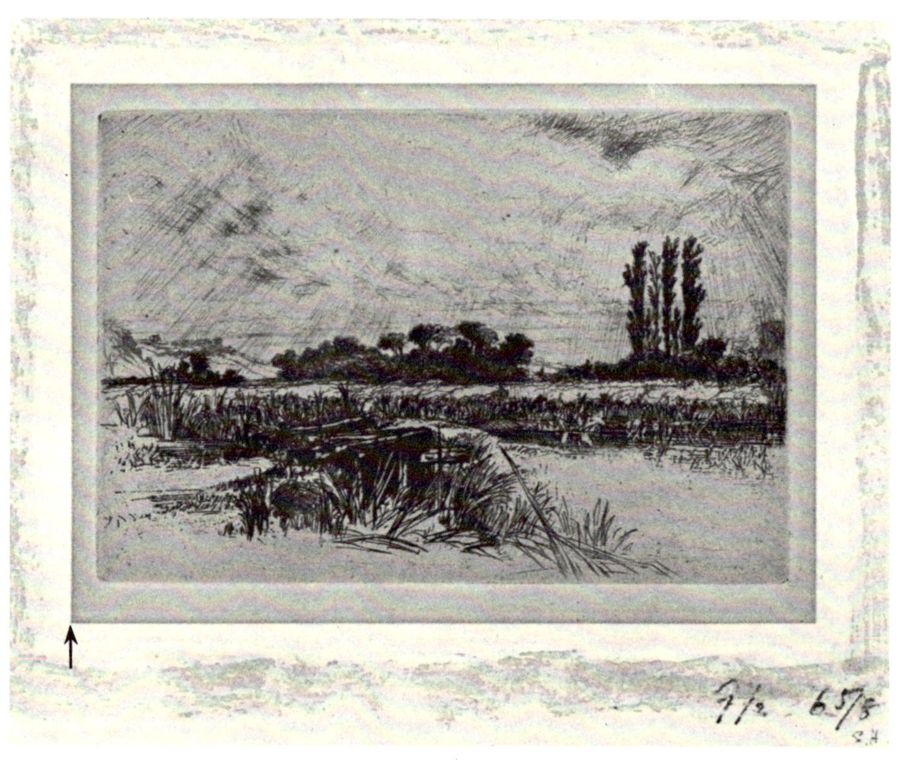

5 *The original mat for this etching was of poor quality and contained corrosive chemicals that caused a dark brown stain coinciding with the opening of the mat (see arrow).*
SEYMOUR HADEN (1818–1910), *A Water Meadow.*

3 · Matting and Framing

MATTING

A mat serves to protect a picture, whether framed or stored, and to enhance its aesthetic qualities. Since the mat is in close contact with the picture, the collector and framer should be particularly careful about the quality of the materials used in its manufacture. False economy leads many inexperienced framers to use wood-pulp matting board, which is acidic and contains a high percentage of unrefined groundwood pulp that inevitably disintegrates. The picture absorbs some of the destructive chemicals and becomes stained. Mat board of this type is usually faced on both sides with a paper of better quality (even pure rag stock may be used) to make the discoloration less apparent. When an opening for the picture is cut, however, the inner core of inferior material is exposed, and the corrosive chemicals soon migrate into the picture. Pictures that have been kept in such a mat for just a few years begin to show a characteristic brown stain that corresponds with the inner edge of the mat opening (Figure 5).

The only safe matting board now available is "museum board," called all-rag matting board,* which is composed not of actual rags but of high-grade cellulose obtained from cotton fibers. It is acid-free and manufactured in only two colors, white and off-white. It can be obtained in three thicknesses: two-ply (approximately 1/32 inch), four-ply (1/16 inch), and eight-ply (1/8 inch). The first is helpful where there is a shortage of storage space, but it should be used only for pictures whose value is not particularly great. The four-ply thickness is the one in most general use and provides an adequate depth to allow for minor buckling of the picture or the relief qualities of some woodcuts, as well as sufficient "breathing space" between the glass and the picture if it is framed. For pastels, collages, and especially large pictures like contemporary lithographs, the eight-ply thickness is recommended. One may substitute two sheets of four-ply, which are somewhat easier to cut and are less expensive than the single sheet of eight-ply.

Museum board is usually sold in quantities of twenty-five sheets measuring 30 (or 32) by 40 inches, but some of the larger art supplies stores sell smaller quantities to customers interested in cutting their own mats. Mats can also be improvised out of heavyweight, hot-pressed watercolor paper.

The basic window mat (see Figure 6) consists simply of two pieces of mat board hinged together with a strip of gummed cloth tape.* A well-proportioned mat should reflect the dimensions of the picture, and its lower margin should be slightly greater than the upper. If placed directly in the mathematical center of the mat, the picture will appear to be just below center, so that a wider bottom margin is needed as compensation. A space of at least 1/8 inch should be allowed around all sides of the image or plate mark. This is particularly important for a print without margins, since, if too little tolerance is allowed, the edges of the print may be damaged when the mat is opened and closed.

The only essential tools for cutting a mat opening are a straightedge made of tough material and a sharp knife, easily obtainable in most art supplies stores. Various devices ranging in price from about five to nearly three hundred dollars are supposed to make it possible for a beginner to cut a professional-looking opening. They perhaps have their place, but for simplicity and versatility the ordinary mat knife, combined with practice, is hard to improve upon.

The difficulty most frequently encountered by those using a mat knife for the first time stems from the tendency to try to cut through the board in one stroke. This tires the arm quickly and makes control of the blade more difficult. Use a light, even pressure and concentrate on keeping the angle of the knife constant. At first, three or four strokes may be necessary to cut through a four-ply thickness, but after some practice only two will be needed, one to make an initial scoring and another, firmer cut to finish. The knife should be held at an angle so as to make a beveled edge around the opening, which is more pleasing visually than an abrupt ninety-degree cut. After the opening is made, the beveled edge itself will be almost knife-sharp and should be lightly sanded to prevent possible damage to the picture. The sharpness of the outer edges of the mat should also be reduced by light sanding or by running the back of the knife along them, especially if the mat is to be kept unframed as part of a study collection. The mat is then more agreeable to handle and less likely to scratch or abrade the surface of another picture if accidently dragged across it.

Hold the picture in position in the mat by attaching it to the backboard, not the front, with two hinges affixed to the upper edge of the reverse side of the picture (see Figures 7 and 8). Never paste the corners of a picture directly to the backboard. Hinging allows the picture to hang freely in the mat and permits the paper to expand or contract without stress as the atmospheric conditions vary. If the picture is likely to be transferred from one mat to

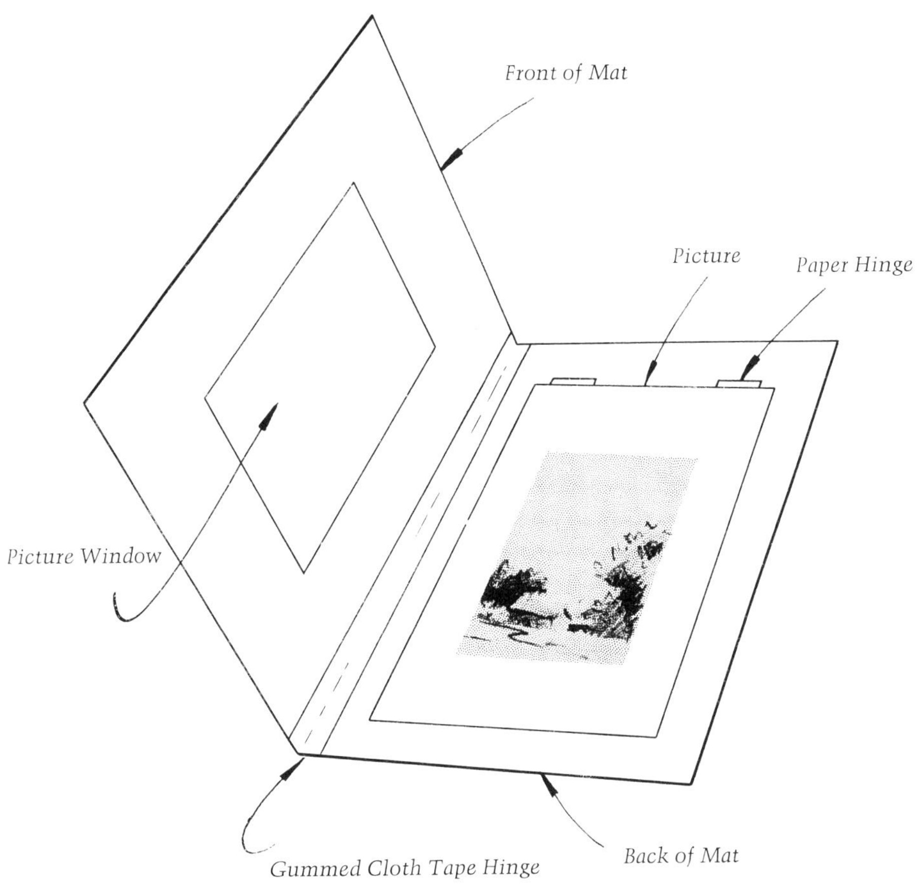
Front of Mat
Picture
Paper Hinge
Picture Window
Gummed Cloth Tape Hinge
Back of Mat

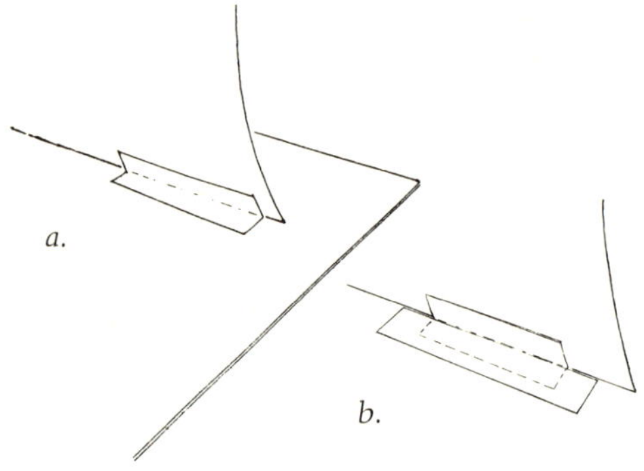

7 Folded Hinges *(must be used if edges of a picture cannot be covered by mat)*
a. simple folded hinge *b. hinge reinforced with strip of paper*

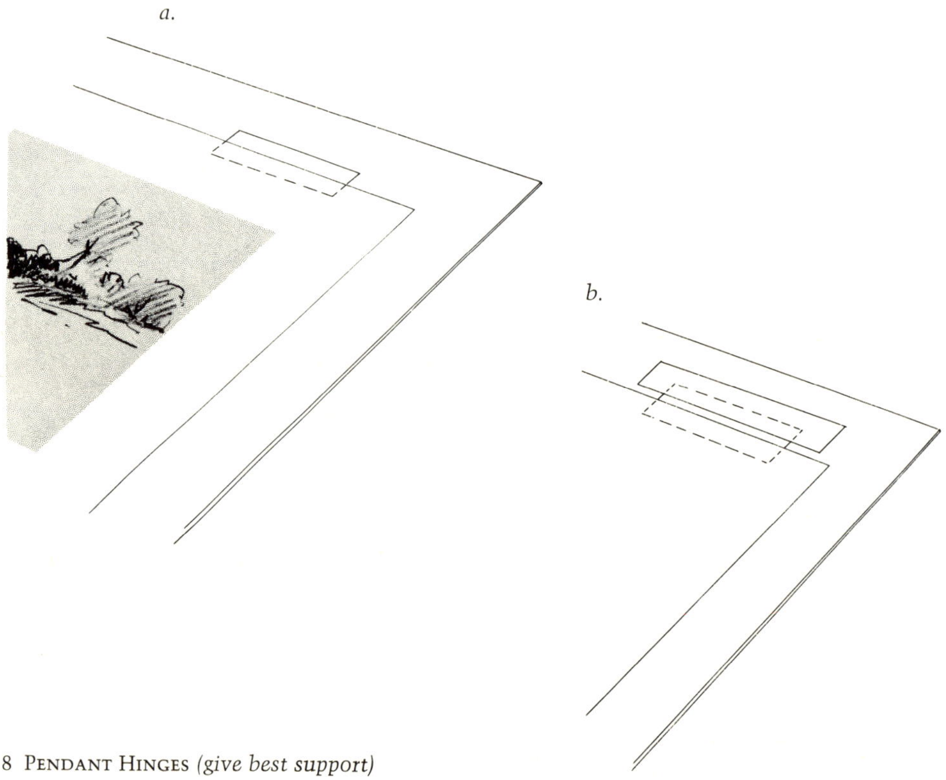

a.

b.

8 Pendant Hinges *(give best support)*
a. for hinges applied with paste
b. for gummed paper hinges or reinforcement of those applied with paste

another, the picture can be hinged to a sheet of rag paper, which in turn is attached to the backboard. When attaching a picture to its mat never use pressure-sensitive tapes of any kind (masking tape, scotch tape, etc.), gummed brown wrapping tape, synthetic glues, or rubber cement. Use instead a good quality gummed paper* or a Japanese paper* applied with starch paste.

Gummed paper may be cut in strips one-half inch in width, of whatever length is demanded by the size and weight of the picture to be supported. The strips are folded in half and applied first to the picture and then to the backboard. For especially large pictures (e.g., contemporary graphics) use short lengths of gummed cloth tape, which is stronger than paper. Gummed paper or cloth hinges are simple and quick to use, can be removed easily, and are less dangerous in the hands of an inexperienced worker than hinges that must be applied with paste. Hinges made of Japanese paper take more time and practice to apply. Select a Japanese paper whose weight matches the picture, and do not apply the paste too thickly or the picture will buckle around the hinge. After attaching the hinges, cover them with blotting paper held down by a light weight for a few hours until they are dry.

The best adhesive for hinges is made from starch, although wheat or rice flour can be substituted. In a two-quart double boiler put four and one-half cups of cold water and one cup of starch. Let it stand for a few minutes to allow the starch to become thoroughly wet. One-eighth of a teaspoon of sodium fluoride may be added as an insecticide, but this chemical is *extremely* poisonous and must be handled with great care. Cook over barely simmering water for twenty to twenty-five minutes, stirring frequently. When ready, it will be thick and opalescent and will be filled with minute air bubbles. At this point one teaspoon of a twenty percent solution of thymol in alcohol may be stirred in; this will preserve the paste for months if kept covered. Cool by placing the top of the double boiler in a bath of cold water, stirring the paste frequently to prevent the formation of lumps.

A hinge should not be wider than necessary for satisfactory adhesion. To keep a picture from slipping in the mat, the length of a hinge, measured along the upper edge of the picture, is more important than its width. It is sometimes said that the hinging paper should be weaker than the picture so that it would give way first if the picture were put under strain, but this requirement cannot be fulfilled in practice. Experience has shown that a picture is more likely to incur damage because of hinges that are too weak rather than too strong. Hinges must be able to withstand the shock of accidental rough handling or dropping of the mat or frame.

Museum board is not now available in the same variety of colors and textures as the inferior wood-pulp types. A colored or decorated mat must be made either by covering the all-rag mat with a high-quality paper of the desired color and texture or by coloring the mat itself. If for some exceptional reason a wood-pulp mat already on the picture has to be saved (if it bears the artist's signature, for example), it can be placed on top of a mat made of all-rag board.

Choosing the color and design of the mat can be either an enjoyable experience or one of utter frustration, depending on the individual. A good rule to follow for both the amateur and professional framer is that a picture should not have to compete for attention with its surroundings. This does not mean, however, that the basic colors in the picture should be repeated in the mat. The glowing brown tones of a bistre drawing, for example, lose their effect if surrounded with a mat of a tan or umber tone. A cool slate blue or olive gray provides a visual complement to the color of the drawing and enhances its appearance. Using complementary colors in this manner is often the key to presenting a picture with its full aesthetic effect.

As a general rule, the off-white color of the all-rag matting board is sufficient for etchings and engravings. Simple, colored mats look well on watercolors, and mats more elaborately decorated with color, ruled lines, and perhaps a narrow strip of gold paper ("French mats") are often effective on drawings. Bear in mind that the simplicity of a mat's appearance is the key to continued enjoyment of the picture.

Several matted pictures can be stored conveniently in wooden drawers or solander boxes, which are the traditional container for matted pictures. This type of box opens out flat, forming a convenient temporary tray, and permits easy access to mats stored within. Large pictures and maps (up to approximately 30 by 40 inches) may be kept matted and in acid-free folders, but in the case of oversize posters and prints individual solutions have to be devised.

FRAMING

The exact style and color of a frame is a matter of personal taste, but the advice of a competent framer will be helpful, since there are a number of hazards. A picture can be damaged by placing it directly against a wooden back. Disfiguring stains often result from resins exuded by the wood itself. If several pieces of wood are used, the openings between them allow pollutants in the air to attack and discolor the picture (see Figure 3). An enterprising individual in the late nineteenth century patented a variation on the wooden back that consisted of thin, narrow strips of wood laminated between two pieces of paper. He might have second thoughts about his invention now if he could see how many pictures it has disfigured. Even if there are no signs of staining, any picture with a wooden back should be opened to make sure it is properly protected with a piece of all-rag board.

Never place a picture directly against the glass, since glass easily condenses moisture and may cause the growth of mold. There is also a chance that the surface of the picture will stick to the glass, resulting in serious damage. A mat creates a "breathing space" between the picture and the glass and allows the picture to move in response to changing atmospheric conditions (see Figure 9). If a mat is not considered desirable, as is sometimes the case with modern prints, the same protection can be provided by a strip of mat board cut sufficiently narrow that it will be hidden beneath the rabbet (inner edge) of the frame. Or Plexiglas may be used instead of glass, since it is a better thermal insulator and will not condense moisture as easily as glass. Plexiglas is unbreakable and is available with colorless additives that filter out ultra-

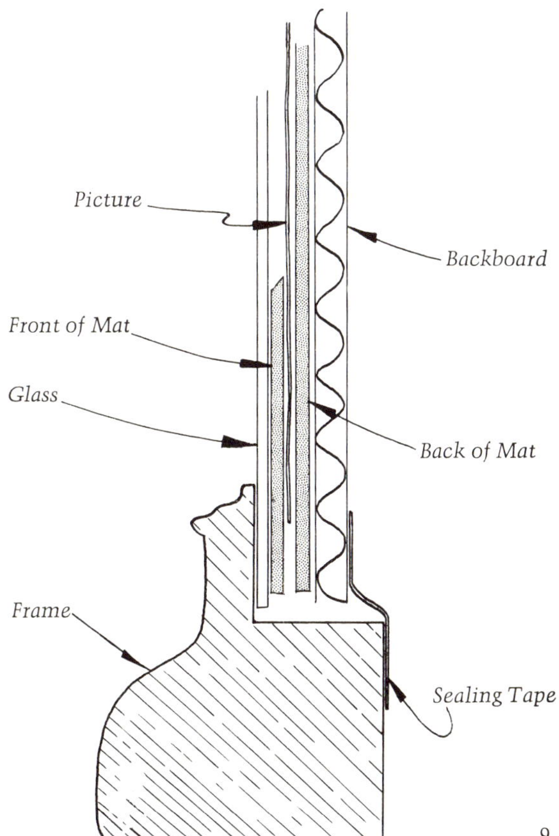

9 Cross Section of a Framed Picture

violet rays.* It is particularly suitable for a picture that has to be transported or subjected to handling that might break the glass. The disadvantages of Plexiglas are that it scratches easily and has a tendency to collect dust because of its inherent static electricity. Minor scratches can be removed with polishing materials now available.* Static electricity may be reduced by using one of the antistatic cleaning solutions formulated for Plexiglas.

To protect a picture from dust, dirt, and flying insects seal the back of the frame with corrugated cardboard, stiff pasteboard, masonite, or featherweight board.* Use nails to secure the board in place, not staples or glazier's points, which soon loosen and fall out. Especially fragile pastels or gouache paintings may be damaged by the shock of hammering the nails. The best method for these is to hold the back in place with metal or wooden braces secured with screws. Seal the gap between the backboard and the frame with gummed wrapping tape, which is permeable to atmospheric moisture and allows the frame to "breathe" and respond to changes in temperature and humidity. A completely airtight seal is neither possible nor desirable, since a significant drop in temperature would cause a dangerous buildup of humidity within the frame. It is better to control the conditions in the room where the picture hangs than to try to burden the frame with that responsibility.

When cleaning a framed picture, never spray the cleaning solution directly onto the surface of the glass or Plexiglas. The liquid may run down inside the frame and stain the mat or cause a dangerous elevation of the humidity inside the frame. Apply the cleaner to the cloth instead.

Never allow the framer to cut or trim the margins of a picture. To do so may damage its aesthetic effect, destroy evidence of authenticity, and in general diminish its desirability and monetary value.

The back of a frame occasionally bears a label that is pertinent to the provenance or authenticity of the picture. If such a label is a document in its own right, it should be treated accordingly and properly protected. If it can be removed from the frame, it may be preserved in an acid-free envelope attached to the rear of the frame, protected from dust by a sheet of cellulose acetate. Or the label could be hinged into the mat itself.

If a picture is kept permanently framed, it is advisable to open and examine it periodically, about every ten years or so, to make sure that it is in good condition. Even if everything is satisfactory, the inner surface of the glass should be cleaned. It is surprising how much of a haze can develop on the inside of a picture glass within just a few years. Sometimes a "ghost" image of the picture appears on the glass, especially in the case of prints, apparently because of the transference of volatile components of the printing ink to the glass.

Pictures should never be framed between two pieces of glass, whether with or without a mat. This method of framing increases the danger of mold growth, and if an object hits the glass, it is likely to pierce the picture and both pieces of glass, thus causing considerable damage. If both sides of a picture or document must be visible, Plexiglas should be used instead of glass.

Never use "nonglare glass" on valuable pictures. To function properly it must be placed directly against the picture, a practice that, as mentioned previously, should be avoided. If it is used with a mat to keep it away from the picture, its frosted appearance makes viewing of the picture difficult. Reflection on glass can be dealt with by appropriate placing of the picture in relation to the light.

Pictures can be hung from molding with hooks and nylon line, which is nearly invisible. The local hardware or sporting goods store can supply line of the proper strength to support the weight of the picture. Another method is to use copper wire painted to match the walls, as is done in some museums. If there is no molding, the usual combination of picture wire, screw eyes, and hooks nailed into the wall will suffice for lightweight frames. A piece of adhesive tape wrapped around the middle of the picture wire will help to keep the picture from tilting. Picture wire exerts tension on each side of the frame, however, and may break apart the corners of heavier frames. They are best hung without wire from two separate wall hooks through the screw eyes. This method does not strain the frame, keeps it level, and gives safer support. Hold the picture against the wall in the desired position (level it with the help of another person), press firmly against the frame, and move it slightly to one side. The screw eyes will leave light marks on the wall, which will help in nailing the hooks.

Gummed or self-adhesive hooks are useful as a temporary support for lightweight, expendable pictures, posters, and other decorations but are not safe for permanent hanging of framed pictures.

To judge by the frequency with which buckling of a picture is mentioned, it is one of the chief causes of concern for the owner. It does not in itself constitute a danger, however, since it is perfectly natural for handmade paper to show some slight degree of movement. If a picture appears to be absolutely flat, it may even be an indication that it has been mounted down. Excessive buckling, however, may be caused merely by too much pressure on the edges of a picture by either the mat or frame and can usually be corrected by the framer. Localized cockling, or puckering, may be caused by the presence of old tape, patches, or glue on the back of a picture, in which case the picture should be brought to a restorer for advice.

Under no condition should a picture be mounted down merely for the sake of removing a few waves or slight buckling, but, unfortunately, this is one of the most common practices today among less-experienced framers and ill-advised collectors. Even Rembrandts have fallen victim to being mounted down on cheap wood-pulp boards with carpenter's glue, photographer's heat-sealing tissue, and synthetic glues. Just as common is the gluing of watercolors onto brown kraft paper and pulling them tight as a drumhead across a wooden stretcher. This method of mounting should be avoided, since the wood resins and cheap paper will cause stains, and because the constant tension on the picture may weaken the fibers of the paper. In certain cases it may be necessary for the purposes of conservation to support a fragile or damaged picture by backing it with a handmade paper, but this operation should be done only by a competent restorer (see "A Note on Restoration"). Gluing pictures down indiscriminately is harmful, unnecessary, and diminishes the monetary and aesthetic value of a work of art. A picture that has been mounted down should be taken to a restorer for advice as to whether it can be removed from its backing.

4 · A Note on Restoration

Restoration is a palliative for the abuse to which paper is subjected, abuse – as the preceding discussion has shown – that can take many forms. The restorer is the doctor. He knows the composition and textures of papers, old and new. He is familiar with the technical basis of applying pigments or ink to paper, and he understands and respects works of art on paper.

If a picture or book is found to be damaged in any of the ways that have been described here, it should be taken to a restorer for examination. He will report on its condition and will suggest possible means of treatment. He will also be able to offer advice on how to prevent further deterioration. He may find that washing, deacidification, and sizing are sufficient remedies. If the paper is brittle or has been weakened by corrosive inks, he may recommend reinforcing it with a thin paper. He can often successfully remove water stains and foxing, so that a picture may again be viewed with pleasure. Restoration has its limitations, but a competent restorer knows them well and will take care to inform the owner of both the limits and risks involved.

The following "case history" of a restoration incorporates most of the problems with paper that have been mentioned in this guide.[1] The restored picture, *Christ on the Cross* (Netherlandish, 1450-1460), is possibly the largest early Flemish woodcut.[2] It was printed in a light brown ink on two sheets of paper that were joined together in the middle of the picture. It was colored by hand and then mounted on a rough panel of unplaned pine 1/4 inch thick. The over-all size of the print is 33 inches by 21 inches.

When brought in for restoration the picture was badly decayed after five hundred years of exposure to atmospheric changes, gases, candle spatterings, dirt, and dust. All these factors contributed to the oxidation, changing, and obscuring of some of the colors as well as to the general decay of the paper on which the woodcut was printed and of the wooden back on which the print was mounted. It had been attacked by silverfish *(Lepisma saccharina)*, and its entire surface was drilled with holes by woodworms. The worms had

1. This report was originally published in *Bulletin of the Museum of Fine Arts*, 49, no. 277, 1951, in an article entitled "Transfer of a Fifteenth-Century Print from Wood to Paper," by Francis W. Dolloff.
2. See Richard S. Field, *Fifteenth-Century Woodcuts and Metalcuts from the National Gallery of Art, Washington, D. C.*, Washington [1965], cat. no. 136.

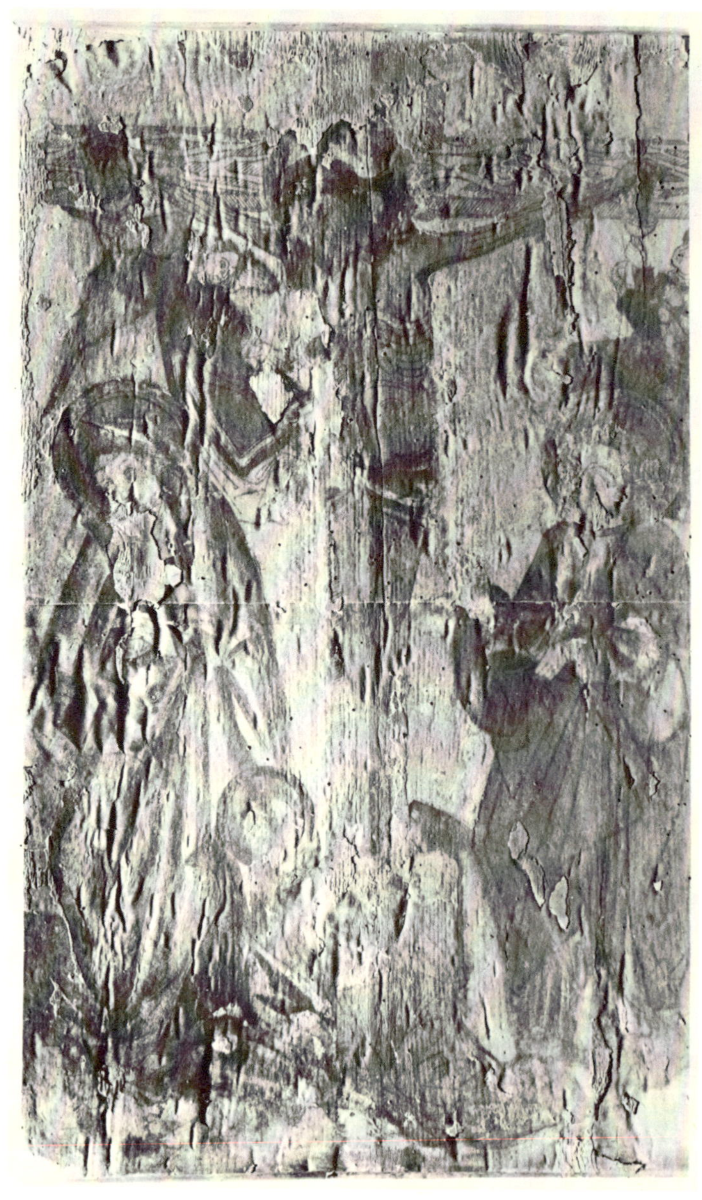

10 *This very early woodcut was extensively damaged by silverfish, woodworms, candle spatterings, and climatic extremes while exposed for centuries as part of a church altar.*
NETHERLANDISH SCHOOL, *Christ on the Cross*, 1450–1460.
(Reproduced by permission of the National Gallery of Art, Washington.)

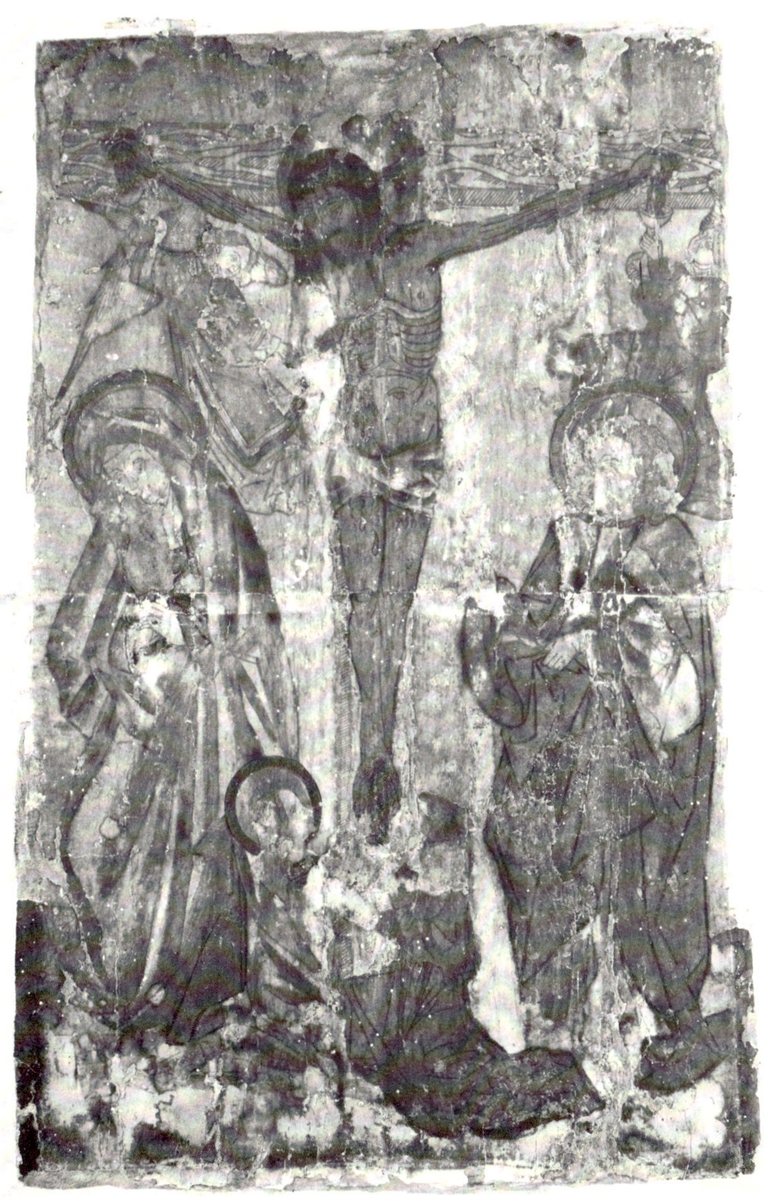

11 *Restoration of the woodcut included removing it from the old wooden panel in dozens of individual pieces, which were replaced in their proper position on a strong sheet of handmade paper.*

eaten so much of the wooden panel and frame that it was hardly more than a shell. The silverfish had eaten from the edge inward, all around, and even into the picture itself. Paper and wood expand and contract at different rates in response to varying atmospheric conditions, and extremes of temperature and humidity had caused the paper to blister or pull away from the panel in many places. These places were very brittle and would have crumbled with even a slight pressure. When the panel had cracked the paper had cracked with it. A white deposit on the surface appeared to be the remains of a protective coating, such as varnish, applied many years ago.

At first examination it was thought that the best that could be done was to remove the dirt and possibly some of the white deposits. This was attempted by careful application of alcohol on cotton swabs rolled over the surface. The picture did clean up slightly and look brighter. But there was still the matter of conservation to be considered. Spraying it with a protective coating would make its removal from the panel difficult, if such an attempt were made. It was left in the laboratory for three months while we gathered courage and ideas for a different approach. One day, after experimenting with moisture on a corner, it was found that the agglutinant would soften readily enough and the paper separate from the panel. The plan of action was laid out.

It was thought that the best material on which to mount the print was a paper as near to the original as possible, and a craftsman of handmade paper in New York was consulted. He used some heirloom linen to make all-rag paper, with deckled edges. Two pieces from the largest mold, 23 by 18 1/2 inches, were joined, as was the original, to make a single sheet. A sample of the fifteenth-century paper had been sent to the craftsman to match for color and texture.

The picture was then photographed in black and white and in color. A scale drawing was made on a heavy board, with the help of a colored slide thrown on a screen. This was done so that, after removal from the panel, the pieces could be returned to their proper position. It was necessary to remove the entire picture from the panel before mounting it on the linen rag paper, because repeated moistening would have varied the amount of stain removed and produced a very uneven look when dried. An outline drawing was made on the linen all-rag paper that was to be the final backing for the picture. Since this handmade paper was fairly soft, it was dipped in sizing made from vellum and while still damp brushed over with mounting-paste made from triple-milled wheat flour.

The operation of removing the picture from the wooden panel was then started. First the panel was placed on a tilted table. Warm water was flowed over the face of the print and left for five minutes. The very delicate work of removing the pieces of paper from the panel to the scale drawing was undertaken. We began with the upper left corner and worked across the top to the right and down to the center where the two pieces were joined together horizontally. This top section came off in about five large pieces. The bottom, which was in a worse state of deterioration, was much more difficult and came off in many, many pieces. The center portion of the Apostle John's robe was in particularly poor condition. St. John's raised right hand was completely eaten away by silverfish. It does not show in the before-restoration photograph because the printed outlines of the fingers were furrowed through to the wooden back.

After the pieces had been removed, they were found to be covered on the back with a thick mucilaginous substance that had been the mountant, and even small splinters from the pine panel were sometimes imbedded in it. Each piece, therefore, had to be cleaned before it could be remounted. In the process of cleaning, the pieces were floated in water and placed on a blotter. The slight pressure used in cleaning the back actually caused some of the surface dirt and stain to come off on the blotter. A certain latitude in manipulation is allowed with old watercolor, because over a number of years of softening and hardening, of expanding and contracting with atmospheric changes, the pigment becomes fixed with the size and cellulose of the paper, so that warm water is not likely to move it.

When the pieces were completely removed from the wooden panel and cleaned, they were mounted one by one to the already prepared linen paper, which was to be the permanent back. With the heavy absorption of water the old paper had expanded, and even with the help of the outline drawing, a great deal of judgment was needed in arranging the pieces. Here the scale drawing proved its value. The entire procedure of removing the woodcut from the wooden panel to mounting it to a new back took two people eight hours. After a week of drying under a stack of blotters, changed several times, the reassembled woodcut was finally put for five minutes under infrared lamps, to assure complete drying. In a few places, where the original paper was missing, touches of color were added to pull the design together. After this, the picture was sprayed with a plastic (poly-vinyl-copolymer) to protect the colors and seal the paper. The restoration and treatment with plastic should prevent further decay and discoloration.

The restoration of this woodcut illustrates that even pictures that are on the brink of total disintegration can sometimes be rescued and preserved by the restorer. But it should also be a reminder that much of the damage that occurs to pictures can be avoided by observing the preventive measures outlined in this guide. If in providing the reader with this set of common-sense rules for preservation the authors enable him to prolong the life of at least one of his treasured pictures or books, their goal will be achieved.

Materials and Services

It is hoped that the following list of materials will be helpful to the reader. The Museum of Fine Arts cannot, however, make any guarantee as to their quality or assume responsibility for their use.

All-rag matting board (museum board)

Andrews/Nelson/Whitehead
7 Laight Street
New York, New York 10013

Charles T. Bainbridge's Sons
20 Cumberland Street
Brooklyn, New York 11205

Owen-Duff Paper Company
465 Cambridge Street
Allston, Massachusetts 02134

Tileston and Hollingsworth Company
211 Congress Street
Boston, Massachusetts 02110

University Products
Cheshire, Massachusetts 01225

Gummed linen tape (Holland tape)

Dennison Manufacturing Company
Coated Paper Division
300 Howard Street
Framingham, Massachusetts 01701

Gane Brothers and Lane, Inc.
1335 West Lake Street
Chicago, Illinois 60607

Gaylord Brothers, Inc.
P. O. Box 61
Syracuse, New York 13201

Gummed transparent hinging tape

Talas
104 Fifth Avenue
New York, N. Y. 10011

Hinges may also be improvised from the gummed flaps of high-quality envelopes, margins of sheets of stamps, or philatelists' hinges.

Japanese papers

Aiko's Art Materials Import
714 North Wabash Avenue
Chicago, Illinois 60611

Andrews/Nelson/Whitehead
7 Laight Street
New York, New York 10013

K.Y.O. Trading Company, Ltd.
Sanjodori, East Jingumichi
Kyoto, Japan

Washi No Mise
5116 Saratoga Avenue, N. W.
Washington, D. C. 20016

Talas
104 Fifth Avenue
New York, New York 10011

Artist's drawing papers

Aiko's Art Materials Import
714 North Wabash Avenue
Chicago, Illinois 60611

Andrews/Nelson/Whitehead
7 Laight Street
New York, New York 10013

Strathmore 100 percent rag Artist Drawing Papers
Strathmore Paper Company
West Springfield, Massachusetts 01089
(Also available in art supplies stores.)

Starch for paste

K. Y. O. Trading Company
Sanjodori, East Jingumichi
Kyoto, Japan

Cover tissue

Esleeck Fidelity onion skin, glazed finish

Esleeck Manufacturing Company
Turners Falls, Massachusetts 01376

Owen-Duff Paper Company
465 Cambridge Street
Allston, Massachusetts 02134

Reflex matte tissue

Process Materials Corporation
329 Veterans Boulevard
Carlstadt, New Jersey 07072

Featherweight board

Backing for framed pictures.

Charles T. Bainbridge's Sons
20 Cumberland Street
Brooklyn, New York 11205

Solander boxes

The Mosette Co.
28 East 22nd Street
New York, New York 10010

Spink and Gaborc, Inc.
32 West 18th Street
New York, New York 10003

Talas
104 Fifth Avenue
New York, New York 10011

Acid-free folders, storage boxes

The Hollinger Corporation
3810 S. Four Mile Run Drive
Arlington, Virginia 22206

Acid-free papers for wrapping, end leaves, lining storage boxes, etc.

Process Materials Corporation
329 Veterans Boulevard
Carlstadt, New Jersey 07072

Talas
104 Fifth Avenue
New York, New York 10011
(Also sells in small quantities.)

Permanent book printing papers ("Superfine" quality)

Carter, Rice, Storrs and Bement, Inc.
273 Summer Street
Boston, Massachusetts 02210

Mohawk Paper Mills
Cohoes, New York 12047

Plexiglas

Type UF-1 reduces the relative damage rate of zenith skylight by an estimated 90 percent of the unfiltered rate, while UF-3 reduces the rate of damage by 95 percent.

Rohm and Haas Co.
Plastics Dept.
Independence Mall West
Philadelphia, Pennsylvania 19105
(Also supplies filters for fluorescent lights.)

Plexiglas polishing cloths

Polysand abrasive cloths
Micro-Surface Finishing Products, Inc.
P.O. Box 249
Burlington, Iowa 52601

Cellulose acetate sheets

Write to the following address for technical information and names of local suppliers:

Eastman Chemical Products, Inc.
Plastics Division
480 Cochituate Road
Framingham, Massachusetts 01702

Bookbinding and library supplies, archival restoration materials

Gane Brothers and Lane, Inc.
1335 West Lake Street
Chicago, Illinois 60607

Gaylord Brothers, Inc.
P.O. Box 61
Syracuse, New York 13201

Talas
104 Fifth Avenue
New York, New York 10011

Leather dressings, potassium lactate solution

Talas
104 Fifth Avenue
New York, New York 10011

Silica gel

For dehumidifying closed containers.

Howe and French, Inc.
99 Broad Street
Boston, Massachusetts 02110

Fungicide (thymol)

Howe and French, Inc.
99 Broad Street
Boston, Masschusetts 02110
(Also found in some pharmacies.)

Paper quality test kit

A set of three prepared chemical indicator solutions which, when applied to paper of unknown composition, show by changes in their color the presence of acidity, ground wood, and alum. Very useful for simple, routine quality control.

W. J. Barrow Research Laboratory, Inc.
428 North Boulevard
Richmond, Virginia 23221

Archivist's pens

A convenient means of detecting acidity in papers of unknown quality. The presence of acidity is shown by color change in a spot of indicator solution applied with the pen.

Process Materials Corporation
329 Veterans Boulevard
Carlstadt, New Jersey 07072

Talas
104 Fifth Avenue
New York, New York 10011

Micro Essential Laboratories, Inc.
4224 Avenue H.
Brooklyn, New York 11210
(Supplies both wide and mid-range indicators.)

Selected Bibliography

Barrow, William J. *Permanence/Durability of the Book*. 6 vols. Richmond, Va.: Dietz Press, 1963–1969.

Clapp, Verner W. "The Story of Permanent/Durable Book-paper, 1115–1970." *Scholarly Publishing*, 2, 1971, pp. 107–124, 229–245, 353–367.

Cunha, G. D. M. *Conservation of Library Materials*. Metuchen, N. J.: The Scarecrow Press, 1967.

"Deterioration and Preservation of Library Materials." *Library Quarterly*, 40, no. 1, 1970, entire issue.

Gallo, Fausta. "Biological Agents Which Damage Paper Materials in Libraries and Archives." *Recent Advances in Conservation*, 1963, pp. 55–61.

Gettens, Rutherford J. and Stout, George L. *Painting Materials: A Short Encyclopedia*. New York: Dover, 1966.

Harrison, Laurence S. *Report on the Deteriorating Effects of Modern Light Sources*. New York: The Metropolitan Museum of Art, 1953.

Horton, Carolyn. *Cleaning and Preserving Bindings and Related Materials*. 2nd ed. rev. Chicago: American Library Association, 1969.

Hunter, Dard. *Papermaking*. 2nd ed. New York: Knopf, 1967.

[International Council of Museums.] *Climatology and Conservation in Museums*. Paris: UNESCO, 1960. (Reprinted from *Museum*, 13, no. 4, 1960.) Covers atmospheric pollution, ideal climatic conditions, and methods of measuring and controlling climatic conditions.

International Council of Museums. *Problems of Conservation in Museums*. Works and Publications, 8. London: Allen and Unwin, 1969. Contains a technical evaluation of the most widely used methods of document lamination.

Ivins, W. M., Jr. *How Prints Look*. Boston: Beacon Press, 1958.

Labarre, E. J. *Dictionary and Encyclopedia of Paper and Paper-Making*. Amsterdam: Swets and Zeitlinger, 1952.

Langwell, W. H. *The Conservation of Books and Documents*. London: Pitman, 1957.

Library of Congress. *Papermaking: Art and Craft*. Washington, 1968.

Mayer, Ralph. *The Artist's Handbook of Materials and Techniques*. 3rd ed. rev. New York: Viking Press, 1972.

Minogue, Adelaide E. *The Repair and Preservation of Records*. National Archives, Bulletin No. 5. Washington, 1943.

Padfield, Tim. "The Control of Relative Humidity and Air Pollution in Showcases and Picture Frames." *Studies in Conservation*, 11, no. 1, 1966, pp. 8–30.

Plenderleith, H. J. *The Conservation of Antiquities and Works of Art*. Oxford University Press, 1956. Covers the fundamentals of restoring works of art on paper.

Santucci, Ludovico. "The Application of Chemical and Physical Methods of Conservation of Archival Materials." In Garry Thomson, ed. *Recent Advances in Conservation: Contributions to the IIC Rome Conference, 1961*. London: Butterworth, 1963, pp. 39–47.

Stolow, Nathan. *Controlled Environment for Works of Art in Transit*. London: Butterworth, 1966. An analytical approach to protection of art works in transport. Contains numerous concrete suggestions for designing the "ideal" container.

Thomson, Garry. "Air Pollution: A Review for Conservation Chemists." *Studies in Conservation*, 10, no. 4, 1965, pp. 147–167.

Thomson, Garry. "A New Look at Color Rendering, Level of Illumination, and Protection from Ultraviolet Radiation in Museum Lighting." *Studies in Conservation*, 6, nos. 2 and 3, 1961, pp. 49–70.

Thomson, Garry, ed. *Recent Advances in Conservation: Contributions to the IIC Rome Conference, 1961*. London: Butterworth, 1963. Contains several useful articles on environmental control and archival conservation.

Toishi, Kenzo. "Humidity Control in a Closed Package." *Studies in Conservation*, 4, no. 3, 1959, pp. 81–87.

Toishi, Kenzo. "Relative Humidity in a Closed Package." In Garry Thomson, ed. *Recent Advances in Conservation: Contributions to the IIC Rome Conference, 1961*. London: Butterworth, 1963, pp. 13–15.

Watrous, James. *The Craft of Old Master Drawings*. Madison: University of Wisconsin Press, 1967.

Zigrosser, Carl, and Gaehde, Christa M. *A Guide to the Collecting and Care of Original Prints*. New York: Crown Publishers, 1965, pp. 99–117.

The following journals frequently contain information and studies of interest to those concerned with the preservation of books, documents, and works of art on paper.

Art and Archaeology Technical Abstracts.
Published semi-annually at the Institute of Fine Arts, New York University, for the International Institute for Conservation of Historic and Artistic Works, London.

Library Quarterly.
Published by the University of Chicago Press.

Restaurator.
International journal for the preservation of library and archival material. Published by Restaurator Press, Postbox 96, DK-1004 Copenhagen K, Denmark.

Studies in Conservation.
Published quarterly by the International Institute for Conservation of Historic and Artistic Works, London.